THE COMMANDMENTS OF HIGHLY SUCCESSFUL LEADERS

LEADERSHIP IN CHALLENGING TIMES

BY TIM L. HOLMAN

P.O. Box 353
NORTH HAMPTON, OHIO 45349
(937) 964-1534

FRONT COVER
DOLORES BOWERS

Library of Congress Catalog Card Number: 96-95360

ISBN 1-57502-398-9

Printed in the USA by

MORRIS PUBLISHING

3212 East Highway 30 • Kearney, NE 68847 • 1-800-650-7888

SPECIAL THANKS TO:

My father and mother who taught me many things about life and leadership.

My daughters Nikki, Jennifer and Michelle who are always there to remind me of the important things in life.

Dolores Bowers who took the time to help organize, type and proof-read this book.

Finally, to my Lord Jesus Christ, the "ultimate leader".

With love I dedicate this book to Becky, my wife,
who is always there to inspire me with her Christian love.

TABLE OF CONTENTS

Commandment:

INTRODUCTION

These are hectic times that we live in. Times that can challenge even a seasoned leader. But it seems that more and more of our leaders fall each year. Today's world needs strong leaders in our families and our organizations.

General Eisenhower used to place a string on a table to demonstrate his philosophy on leadership. He would say leadership is like this string. Pull it and it will follow, push it and it will become disaligned and go nowhere. Pull the people and they will follow; push them and they will go nowhere.

Jesus was a great example of leadership. He was constantly challenged and responded in a strong confident manner. Jesus demonstrated that service was the highest form of leadership. He taught others how to succeed. And he walked the talk.

Jesus lived in difficult times. He was not accepted by all but he stayed focused on the job at hand. He was constantly seeking ways to help others succeed. Jesus based everything on the solid word of God. The *TEN COMMANDMENTS OF HIGHLY SUCCESSFUL LEADERS* uses the principles set down by our Lord to develop leaders in challenging times.

In many of my management seminars I have been told that God's word has no place in leadership today. Those principles are out dated. They just can't work in today's organizations. Well, I ask those same people to hear me out and try what they learn in the program. As a result there are many organizations out there today succeeding because they are driven by God's word. And God's word is never wrong.

The *TEN COMMANDMENTS OF HIGHLY SUCCESSFUL LEADERS* will help you develop a new attitude. It will give you the skills needed to pull the people that you lead. The heart of any organization is the people. Without the people there is no organization. Treat the members of the organization as the most valuable resource and they will help you and the organization reach new heights of success.

This book is designed to be used in conjunction with the Bible. Each commandment is related to a Scripture. Read the Scripture first then read the chapter in the book. FOCUS on one commandment at a time. Ask your family and your peers at work to help you accomplish these principles. This is a process that will take time to evolve. So be patient. Feel free to contact us if you have questions. Write us and let us know how you're doing.

Each day approach your leadership with these two concepts in mind:

1. Your #1 goal is to help the people succeed because if the people succeed, the organization (or the family) will succeed; and if the Organization succeeds, you as the leader succeeds.

2. Next pray. Each and every day pray frequently. Pray for wisdom, direction and the ability to keep an open mind. You see, God has the answers we're looking for. We just don't take the time to listen. With God on your side you can't help but to succeed.

Commandment #1

HAVE A CLEAR VISION AND MISSION

• •

"Where there is no vision the people will perish."

Proverbs 29:18

Read: 1 Corinthians 10:23-33

VISION:

A successful leader must have a well defined vision of where the organization is going. Think about it. If the leader has no idea what the organization is to become, he or she cannot expect the people to know. No vision causes disalignment and confusion among the members of the organization.

Vision is a picture of where you as a leader intend to take the organization. This picture should be very vivid in your mind. It is distinct and unique because it belongs to you. It is usually far off in the distance but it is as clear in your mind as if it were a present day reality.

Vision is in direct proportion to accomplishment. The more you envision, the more you will achieve. Many corporations today enjoy success because their leader had a vision of that success.

A vision is a dream that is turned into reality. It is a blueprint within the mind that you constantly work to bring into existence. Without first a vision, nothing can be.

Vision gives us a sense of purpose. It is what we are constantly striving for and we know society as a whole will be much better because of it. Vision gives meaning to our mission, our goals and our objectives. Without vision, the leader cannot lead. Simply put, you cannot lead where you cannot see.

Vision is like a compass. It constantly points the way to the future. Without vision the leader becomes lost. When the leader is lost, the followers will become lost as well.

No vision is ever too grand. You must reach for your highest aspirations because it is much better to aim high and miss your target then to aim low and make it.

Vision is what creates tomorrow. Without vision everything becomes stagnant and without meaning. Your vision will determine your destiny, so make it great and move to the next dimension of success.

Vision reaches beyond that which is. It explores that which could be. It's a dream that becomes destiny only when it is sought after. Vision is like a magnet, constantly pulling you closer to the success of making it real.

Walt Disney had a dream. His dream was called *Disney World.* Some say that it was a shame that Walt Disney never saw the completed Disney World but those that knew him well will tell you that Walt Disney saw Disney World long before it was created, because he had created it in his mind. That is vision.

As you begin developing your vision, consider these questions, giving each one serious thought.

PERSONAL VISION:

1. What is the most important aspect in my life?

_____.

2. What do I want to do with my life?

_____.

3. What do I want people to remember about me?

_____.

4. What gives my life meaning?

_____.

5. What opportunities does the future hold?

_____.

ORGANIZATIONAL VISION:

1. What would the ideal organization look like?

_____.

2. What future opportunities are there for the organization?

_____.

3. What kind of people would make up this organization?

_____.

4. When could the organization become the ideal organization?

_____.

5. What do I need to do to make it an ideal organization?

_____.

After considering these questions, write down a brief statement that reflects your vision, both personal and organizational:

_____.

My personal vision:

_____

_____.

My vision of the organization:

_____.

Now share your vision with other members of the organization. Talk about it frequently. Let everyone know where you are going. Vision equals a focused future. It will act as a strong motivator. Vision is the driving force for the successful leader.

MISSION:
Like the vision, the mission statement gives the successful leader a sense of direction and purpose. For years, corporations have relied on their mission statement to give an individual direction, focus and purpose. In essence, it is your agenda in life. Whether you are developing a personal mission or a corporate mission, the process is much the same. In this book we will discuss mainly the individual mission.

A mission statement can be a tool in giving the leader meaning to his or her daily activity. How often do you perform a list of tasks but you are unable to see the meaning behind them? Without a well-defined mission, you become less effective in moving towards your vision.

A typical mission statement should be a short, concise statement that reflects the purpose, values and practices of the leader. There is true power in writing the mission statement down and reviewing it on a regular basis. It is not enough to read it, you must be committed to it and live it. Your mission will keep you aligned with both your vision and your values.

Developing a personal mission statement takes time and energy. Done properly, however, it will keep you moving closer to your vision. As you begin thinking about a mission statement, consider the following:

What is your basic purpose in life? Everyone has certain skills and knowledge. What are your strong points? How can you put these skills to work to make your vision a reality? What makes you feel good? What gives your life meaning?

Values play an important part in developing a mission statement. Your values are the very foundation of you as a leader. Values are the basic beliefs for which you live your life. By including your personal values in your mission statement, you will stay on track. You should never have to compromise your values to accomplish your mission. Doing so will jeopardize your integrity.

How many leaders do you know that have at some point sold out to gain success? Don't be tempted. Stay true to your values and you will always be able to keep your head high. Values are what you stand for and if you don't stand for something, you're sure to fall for anything.

Put your mission statement in writing and keep it with you. Review it frequently so it becomes a constant reminder as to why you are here. I have my mission statement in my daily planner. I can refer to it easily and it helps me stay focused on those things that are most important to me. Other people I know write their mission on a small card and then laminate it. They carry it in their pocket so they can refer to it on a daily basis.

Your mission must be meaningful so that you believe in it and you work to accomplish it. Every activity that you engage in should be supported by your mission. No longer will you ask yourself, "Why am I doing this?".

Who, what, where and why are questions that the mission statement should answer. If your statement answers these questions, you're probably right on track.

_____.

My personal mission:

_____.

ORGANIZATIONAL MISSION:

Mission statements for organizations can be developed much the same way as the personal mission. It is, however, a good idea to obtain input from all the members of the organization. This gives the people ownership in the mission and they are then likely to promote and live it.

To obtain input, the members can be surveyed using questionnaires or in meetings. The important thing to remember is give them a chance to participate in developing this important document.

Once the mission statement is completed, you will need to make it visible. This can be accomplished by having the statement typeset and framed. You may even want each member to sign the document to give it more meaning.

In one organization that I worked, the mission statement was placed on a large 4 x 6 foot banner. When you walked in the door, the first thing you would see is the mission.

I discovered how powerful a mission statement can be when I overheard one front-line employee telling another front-line employee that he was off track. He pointed to the mission statement and said, "See the word *Teamwork*? You're not doing that and it makes a hardship on all the rest of us". The other employee responded, "You're right and I need to change".

Now think about it. Here we have a counseling session taking place, but not between a supervisor and employee. Instead, we have one employee counseling the other. This is a good example of both peer pressure and ownership within the organization.

Properly developed, a mission statement can take the organization to new heights.

PROGRESS NOTES

Commandment #2

SET SMART GOALS

• •

"The laborer's appetite works for him; his hunger drives him on."
Proverbs 16:26

Read: 1 Corinthians 9:24-27

Imagine for a moment a football game. Both teams are on the field, ready to move the ball. The offense snaps the ball and the quarterback stops. He notices that the field has no yard lines or goal lines. Which way should he run? How much progress is he making? How does he know what it takes to score a touchdown? Frustration develops in the quarterback and the game has little meaning.

Our lives can be much like that football game if we don't set and accomplish goals. Without goals, we go through our daily activities performing many tasks, but what purpose do these tasks represent?

The successful leader cannot achieve if he or she has no goal. The vision remains just a dream and success is never grasped. Goals are what place our dreams into action. Without goals you will wander around just trying to survive. Setting and accomplishing goals will allow you to thrive as a leader.

For a goal to be reached, it must be SMART. This acronym stands for Specific, Measurable, Achievable, Realistic and Time-dimensioned.

A specific goal is one that is well defined. It describes exactly what needs to occur for the goal to be met or exceeded. It paints a vivid picture as to what steps lead to success. Specific goals are very distinct in what they say. Anyone should be able to pick up the goal statement and know what it means.

Next, the goal needs to be measurable. This can be done in two ways. Setting a specific date for a goal to be reached makes it measurable. If everything is accomplished by the deadline, we know the goal was met. If the due date arrives and the goal has not been completed, you know the goal was not reached.

Specific numbers can also be used to measure your goal. *I will present four team building seminars by December 31, 1996.* This goal is measurable both by date and a specific number.

By making a goal measurable, it is easy to track your progress in achieving the goal. It allows you to make needed adjustments so you can meet the goal as it was intended.

The next step is to make sure that the goal is achievable. It makes very little sense to set a goal that is so far from reach that it cannot be met. Unachievable goals set you up for failure, frustration and discouragement.

I will complete my Master's degree within six months from today's date. This goal is specific and measurable but if I have not taken graduate classes, this goal is unachievable. On the other hand, if I were to set a goal that states: *I will complete my Master's degree in business administration within three years of today's date*; then this goal is achievable.

Goals need to be obtainable but that doesn't mean that we should make them so easy that accomplishing them has little impact on our vision or mission. It's far better to aim high and miss than to aim low and hit it.

It is also important to make sure your goal is realistic. Setting a goal to walk on the moon would not be realistic for most of us. If the goal fails to be realistic, we will be unable to achieve it. This can lead to a sense of failure and a fear to try again. Make yourself stretch but keep it realistic.

As I stated earlier, a time dimension can be a way to measure your goal. Without a time frame, the goal becomes just a wish. Placing a time limit helps to motivate you towards the accomplishment of the goal. You are able to keep score on your progress. Time limits also allow you to reach the goal early, which acts to motivate you towards setting other goals.

Once you have set smart goals, you will need to break each goal down into objectives. Objectives are small tasks that, when completed, provide you with an accomplished goal. The objectives that are set for each goal are the tasks that are brought into your daily activity. As you plan your day, week or month, bring these objectives into your normal routine. As you accomplish them one by one, you move closer and closer to success.

Examples:

Goal: I will read ten books by January 1, _____.

Objective: 1. Develop a book list by_date_.

2. Go to library to obtain library card by_date_.

3. Read at least 12 pages per day._ongoing._

After reviewing this simple example, you can see how easy it would be to accomplish this goal. That's because we have broken it down into small pieces. Take each objective one at a time and you're sure to succeed.

Now, let's say that my year deadline has arrived but I have only read eight books this year. That's two short of my original goal, so I'm a failure. Right? Wrong! Chances are, if I had never set this goal, I would be like most people who only wish they would read more. So I fell short. I still read eight books. That's great! Now I set another goal for the next year, only this time I may want to shoot for twelve books.

The important thing to remember is that even if you fall short of your goal, you probably made some progress. Progress means you are moving forward and that's just what you need to do if you want to reach your vision.

Whether you are the leader of a large organization or a family of four, goals are what turn dreams into realities.

PROGRESS NOTES

Commandment #3

SHOW INTEGRITY IN ALL THAT YOU DO

• •

"God praises Job because Job maintained his integrity, even though his faith was tested and he suffered greatly."
Job 2:3

Read: Proverbs 11:1-31

Do you have integrity? Try this experiment: Think of a good friend. Now go to the store and buy this person a lottery ticket. Keep it a secret. Don't tell anyone what you have done. You are the only one who knows this lottery ticket is for your friend. Keep the ticket until after the drawing.

Now let's make it more interesting. Let's say the ticket matched the winning number and it is worth 12 million dollars. What do you do? Remember you are the only one that knows you bought this ticket for a friend. Would you give your friend the money or would you keep it? Answer this question and you will have also answered the question about your integrity.

You see, trust and integrity are very different. It is much easier to be honest with other people because they will hold you accountable; but being honest with yourself means that you must make yourself accountable. Frequently you will find yourself saying, "Who will know? I can keep this money and no one will ever know the difference."

Maintaining integrity is more difficult when the stakes are high. If that lottery ticket was worth 20 dollars instead of 12 million dollars, chances are that we would all maintain our integrity by giving the money to our friend.

Think for a moment about the integrity of a steel beam. Left alone the beam will maintain its integrity and stand straight, rigid and strong. But what happens when heat and pressure are applied to the beam? Slowly it will begin to bend. It starts losing its integrity. The more heat and pressure that is applied, the more it bends, thus the more integrity it loses.

In any leadership position, heat and pressure is frequently received. The successful leader can and will withstand this force. His or her integrity stands firm.

VALUES:

How does the successful leader withstand such forces? How is integrity maintained during high levels of heat and pressure?

Maintaining integrity during difficult times requires identifying, defining and living certain values. Now I'm not about to tell you what values you should or should not have, but I will tell you that highly successful leaders have a strong value base. These values are also accompanied by good ethical considerations. Good Christian values provide a very strong foundation that everyone should consider.

Everyone has certain values that are at the center of their life. Most will agree that they possess values but few have taken the time to identify and reflect on them.

Think about a successful leader that you know. What values do they live by? Honesty? Justice? Positive Attitude? Cooperation? There is a different relationship between values and success as a leader. Reflect for a moment on your values. Are you living them?

EXAMPLES OF VALUES:

Honesty	Freedom	Generosity
Justice	Growth	Cooperation
Innovation	Security	Courage
Family	Understanding	Happiness
Health	Financial Security	Fulfillment
Humbleness	Teamwork	Peace
Love of God	Positive Attitude	Success
Intellect	Service	Simplicity
Excellence	Truth	Quality
Life	Mercy	Humor

Most of your values have been instilled within you at a very early age. Your parents, grandparents, teachers and other people who have had a significant influence on your life have helped develop your values. As you think about each of your values you will probably be able to tell from where they have come.

It's also common for certain values to change throughout your life. Some will become higher priorities, while others will decrease in significance. A value centered around family will most likely look different for a father of five compared to that of a bachelor. Financial security may take on a totally different look when you are 50 years old compared to when you were 20.

Writing down your values and describing what each one looks like will help you focus on that which is most important to you. Reviewing them from time to time, like your vision, will prevent you from straying off course in your journey to success. Your integrity will be maintained even when the strongest of forces try to bend you.

Take time to list some of your values below. Then write a definition as to what this value means to you.

MY VALUE: MY VALUE DEFINITION:

_____   _____

                           _____

_____   _____

                           _____

_____   _____

                           _____

_____   _____

                           _____

Compromising your integrity will sooner or later result in some type of punitive consequences. As a successful leader, you must refuse the easy path and concentrate on the ethical path. Your integrity, good or bad, will live on long after you die.

PROGRESS NOTES

Commandment #4

TAKE RESPONSIBILITY FOR ALL YOUR ACTIONS

• •

"Do what is right in the eyes of everyone."
Romans 12:17-18

Read: Psalm 119

Consider for a moment that you are a leader of a large manufacturing company. Your company produces a product that is found to be defective and unsafe. Millions of dollars have been invested in this product. As the product was being produced, you stayed close to the project and worked with engineers to assure that it would go to market ahead of schedule.

Now customer complaints are flooding in. The news media have picked up on the story and the company is receiving a lot of bad press. The board of directors are also upset. How would you handle this situation?

Few people want to admit that they are wrong, but the highly successful leader sees this as a must. You must learn from your mistakes, admit them and go on.

One of the easiest ways out of a situation such as the one described above is to shift the blame elsewhere. The lead engineer, the research and development people or vice president over the division are all good targets for shifting responsibility. You call a press conference and admit the product was faulty and that several key positions in the organization are responsible. These individuals have been fired and the project will be reorganized with all defective problems corrected.

Sounds simple. You took the bull by the horns and corrected the problem swiftly and effectively. You become the hero. Right?

The successful leader becomes successful by supporting others. This means that when you do something wrong, you admit it. Sit down with the people and tell them that you take responsibility. Sure, you can shift the responsibility and you may even look good in the process. The problem is, you are the leader. Good or bad, you are responsible, so stand tall, take the responsibility and all the bad press that comes with it. In the long run you will gain much more respect from others.

I believe in teamwork, but every team has a leader. When our team succeeded, I would praise their efforts. When the team would fail, we would all accept the responsibility for the failure, but as the leader I would always try to take just a little more responsibility than the rest of the team.

If a professional basketball team has a losing year, the owner doesn't fire the team. Instead, the coach (leader) is usually terminated. Why? Because he is responsible for his team's actions, good or bad.

As a leader of my team I'm responsible for the team's actions. Granted, they are responsible as well but I'm ultimately responsible for providing focus, education, training, coaching and for bringing the group together as a cohesive team.

So maybe I failed along the way, which resulted in their failure. So I must take responsibility, or at least part of it, and change that which is in error. Then we move on. We must learn from our mistakes, change and start fresh.

Accepting responsibility for your actions builds trust within the group. People will see you as someone who has nothing to hide. This will go a long way in building good working relationships with others. The comfort level with those associated with you will be enhanced. You will also find that communications will improve as well, since people will have more trust in you. You are human and you are allowed to make mistakes. That is, as long as you learn from those mistakes. Start developing the attitude that there is no such thing as mistakes, just lessons in education.

Taking responsibility for your actions shows that you are confident and comfortable with yourself as a person. You send a clear message that you are human and you can make mistakes too. By being human, people will tend to relate to you with more ease and confidence. You are respected and eventually you will find that the people will go to bat for you and defend you from time to time.

I used to manage a department of about fifty people. All-in-all we had a good team, but two things needed to change. First, I didn't want to be just a manager. I wanted to be a true leader. Second, I didn't want us to be just a good team. I wanted us to be an excellent team. So the redesigning process began.

The first thing that I did was to break the fifty members of the department into three groups. Each group was scheduled for an eight hour retreat at a local hotel. The supervisors were not allowed to attend any of these sessions. I had planned a separate session for them.

Next, the ground rules were set for the retreats. They were very simple. Say what's on your mind. Answer questions honestly. Don't feel threatened for doing so.

Day one came with about eighteen people in attendance. We talked for awhile about the successes of the department over the past two years. We made a list of all our accomplishments on a flip chart and the list grew to about 25. I praised them for their efforts and then we took a short break. Everyone was feeling pretty good about the team and many positive comments were overheard during the break.

When the group came back together, I again reinforced the many accomplishments they had made. Then I said that one thing had to change. I remained silent for about two minutes. Do you know how long two minutes is when no one is talking? You could have heard a pin drop. Everyone was thinking about what needed to change. I then broke the silence by saying, "That one thing is me as a leader. For this team to progress, I need to do better as a leader."

I wish you could have seen their faces! They were sure that I was going to say that they needed to change. Instead, I took the responsibility for my actions and stated that I wanted to be a better leader.

What took place next was probably one of the hardest things I have ever done. I asked the question, "What about my leadership do you dislike? What can I do to change?"

For the next six hours, I listed all of their concerns on a flip chart. Not all the comments were bad. In fact many were very supportive, but I still had a list of over thirty items that they disliked about my management style.

At the end of the day, I thanked everyone for their honesty and I took the responsibility for changing. I asked them not to discuss the retreat with the other two groups and they agreed.

The second and third day went much like the first. We developed a list that totaled nearly one hundred items. Some of which were pointed towards the supervisors.

Now I have to tell you that to spend nearly twenty-four hours listening to people tell me all the things that I was doing wrong was not easy. The only thing that got me through the ordeal was that I had a true desire and commitment to change from a manager to a leader.

Several weeks later, I met with the supervisors at another retreat just for them. We took all of the flip chart sheets and taped them on the wall. Next, we began sorting through the comments to weed out duplicates and to combine those that were similar. When we finished, we had five statements that addressed all of the concerns of the people.

The next step was to take these statements back to the people for their review. They all agreed that if these five things were changed, the department would be much more successful.

An action plan and time schedule was then developed. This too was reviewed with the people for their approval. We would commit to completing the action plan within one year.

Now during the course of all these meetings, I observed something. The communication lines were much more open now than compared to the past. People began trusting me more and they appeared more enthusiastic. You see, they now understood that I was really committed to improving as a leader. They also knew that there were no repercussions for saying what was on their minds. They were convinced that I was sincere in making the department better and that I had no hidden agendas.

It turned out that the action plan was completed in six months. I then surveyed the members of the department and they agreed that all their concerns were addressed.

Now you're probably asking yourself, "How much more successful did the department become?" First, we utilized a team survey instrument that we purchased to determine team effectiveness. This is a nationally recognized survey. Within 18 months, our score went from 158 to 209 (the national average is 152).

Next, the department decreased operational costs by 28% and employee turnover was reduced from 21% to less than 2%. All of this was done within a twelve month period. The team also exceeded organizational goals three years in a row.

By taking responsibility for my actions and by taking some of the heat off of the team, they were able to excel to great levels. Keep in mind, most of the credit for the success must go to the team, not to the leader. They did the work. I just provided the ten commandments of highly successful leaders.

RESPONSIBILITY CHECK:

Do you get defensive when you are criticized?

Do you learn from your mistakes and start fresh?

Are you comfortable in admitting when you make a mistake?

Do you try to hide your weaknesses?

How do you feel when you make a mistake?

How does it make you feel when others know you made a mistake?

PROGRESS NOTES

Commandment #5

PROMOTE EDUCATION AND INNOVATION

● ●

"He who scorns instruction will pay for it, but he who respects a command is rewarded."

Proverbs 1 3:13

Read: Proverbs 13:1-25

EDUCATION:

The successful leader is constantly teaching, mentoring and coaching the people. To be successful, the people need information. There should be no secrets except for those associated with discipline. People cannot be effective at making decisions if they don't have the proper information.

A friend of mine once said that he was constantly teaching his employees everything he knew about the organization. He said he would eventually educate himself out of his job. When I asked why, he said that the day would come when his boss would retire. "When he does, I want that job. So I'm going to have many people ready to take my place." Then he said, "Administration can't use the excuse that there is no one to take my place." Today, he is the president of that company.

As a successful leader, you must empower and delegate employees to do many tasks. If you as a leader don't educate them and provide them with the same information that you have, you are setting them up for sure failure.

Good decisions are based on accurate facts. Without accurate information, quality decision-making is not possible. Remember, the people you lead are a direct reflection on you. So don't you want them to succeed?

BUDGET:

Budget information should be open to all your associates. How can the people be expected to control costs if they have no idea what the budget looks like?

As a leader, you should teach the people about the budget process. Get their input and discuss both revenue and expense issues. Make the budget visible. If organizational policy prohibits this, then share line items that the organization will approve. The budget should not be a big secret. The more the people know about the budget, the more ownership they will have. Along with ownership comes the process to help the organization succeed.

When I was a department director, I would let my associates help form the departmental budget. In one of our budget meetings, I told them that the organization expected us to cut operating expenses by 4%. They began discussing this issue and when they were finished, they announced that they felt they could cut expenses by 10% and not affect operations.

I've got to tell you that I was more than a little nervous with this goal but what made it work was the fact that they had the ownership and they would make it happen. Twelve months later, the department did not cut cost by 10%. Instead, they had reduced operational expenses by 28%! Not bad for a group that was still learning about the budget process.

TEAM BUILDING:

Another key area leaders need to educate the people is that of team building. By learning to function as a team, the organization can become much more effective in their endeavors.

Such things as group dynamics, meeting skills, communication skills and conflict management help the people accomplish more with less difficulty.

There are many programs available to help build teams. I didn't have the money budgeted for this type of program at the time, so I designed my own team building program. It proved very successful and our results were measurable.

One word of caution about team building. It needs to be an ongoing process. Otherwise, left alone, it will revert back to its original form.

PROBLEM SOLVING:

Problem solving techniques will help employees find solutions for situations on the spot. Instead of bringing every problem to the leader, the employee will be able to solve issues in less time and be more productive. This is not to say that every problem that comes up will be solved by the employee but the majority should be handled by them, as much as possible.

By teaching individuals to solve problems, they will feel more needed and their job will become more meaningful. This can pay off in big dividends in quality, productivity and cost containment.

OTHER EDUCATIONAL TOPICS:

Quality improvement, customer relation, quality tools, innovation, the list can go on and on. The point is, you as the leader must assure that your people are constantly growing. Continue to introduce them to new information. Challenge them to learn more and to take on additional responsibility. Then watch how they grow as an asset to the organization.

WAYS TO EDUCATE:

There are many ways that you can provide education to your people. Depending on your budget, you may want to send them to local seminars and workshops. Some universities have outreach programs. You may even want to bring programs in-house so everyone gets the same information at the same time.

Now you may not have money budgeted for education. If this is true, you should do everything in your power to change it. In the mean time, you can take a few minutes on a regular basis to do one-on-one mentoring. Go to the library and pick up some books on a specific topic that you feel would be helpful. Read the book and then have your employees read it. Set aside time to discuss the book. You may want to do the same thing with magazine articles. In any case, this is an inexpensive way to enhance your people's knowledge and skills.

A spin-off advantage to mentoring is the time you get to spend one-on-one in small groups. This shows you honestly care about them and you want them to succeed.

There's an old saying that goes like this:

If you give a man a fish, he will eat once.

If you teach a man to fish, he will eat for the rest of his life.

So teach them everything you can.

PROMOTING INNOVATION:

Innovation and creativity are key elements needed if the organization is to grow. For this reason, the leader must promote and encourage it. Giving an individual the opportunity to try their ideas and helping them to expand on future possibilities helps the organization to be proactive and less likely to become stagnate.

Innovation starts with creativity. Since creativity is an individual process, the leader must bring groups together to develop creative ideas. Innovation can help solve problems within the organization and develop new strategies and new products.

By promoting innovation, the leader can effectively move the company to new levels of success. So you should constantly be looking for the entrepreneurial types in your organization.

THINKING IT OVER

What did you try to do today that was new and different?

When was the last time you spent 30 minutes daydreaming?

Look at things around you. How could you improve them?

What did you learn today?

What did you teach others today?

What books have you read lately?

What skills do you have that you could teach others?

PROGRESS NOTES

Commandment #6
ALLOW MISTAKES

• •

"They will soar on wings like eagles"

Isaiah 40:31

Read: Proverbs 24:1-34

My grandmother once told me a story about two seeds of corn. Both had just recently been planted. The first seed was excited and wanted to sprout his roots, stretch through the topsoil and reach for the warm Spring sun.

The second seed was afraid to sprout its roots because he didn't know what would await him in the deep dark soil; and if he were to press through the topsoil, he may be a sacrifice to the birds or other animals.

So, the first seed grew and became a prize stalk of corn that produced many ears of tasty corn, fulfilling his purpose in life; but the other seed did nothing. Afraid to grow, he just sat there and was later eaten by a crow.

This story illustrates how many people live their lives. They are so afraid of making a mistake, that they do nothing. They live in a shell, constantly in fear of breaking away.

Think back for a minute to when you were in grade school. If you made a mistake, what would happen? The teacher would likely make a big deal of it. After being criticized over and over, you tend to grow up thinking that you are not allowed to make mistakes.

My philosophy on this matter is somewhat different. I tell my children that it's okay to make a mistake, providing you do two things. First, you must learn from the mistake and do everything you can to keep it from happening again. Second, you must always put forth 100% effort. If they have done both of these things, then the mistake becomes a valuable tool for learning, and they will always be willing to step out and take a risk.

Now when I talk about mistakes I am referring to people trying new things, being innovative, stepping out of the confines of their boxes and investigating new possibilities.

Some mistakes are due to poor performance. In this case, you must counsel the individual and get them back on track. For the individual who wants to try a new approach or to work on a new process, mistakes must be allowed and downplayed.

I refer to mistakes as lessons in education. By approaching them in this manner, people tend to look at the process, break it down, improve upon it and try again.

Thomas Edison tried over 5,000 different elements for the light bulb before he found the right one. When asked by a friend, "How can you keep trying after 5,000 failures?", Mr. Edison responded by saying, "I have not failed 5,000 times. I just found 5,000 elements that won't work." Soon after this, he was successful at inventing the light bulb. Where would we be today if Edison would have had a boss who wouldn't allow mistakes?

I have a friend who owns a small business. Each month they have a staff meeting. At these staff meetings every employee is encouraged to bring a mistake that they had made during the past month. They explain what they did wrong, what they had learned and what they plan to do in the future.

My friend then pays cash rewards for the top three best mistakes of the month. He will tell you that this has done more to move his company forward than anything else he can think of.

When people are making mistakes, they are trying new ideas or approaches. They are thinking, learning and becoming innovative. As a leader, you must allow mistakes and you will reap many benefits for doing so.

Let's look at baseball for a few moments. What kind of a batting average must a player have to reach the Hall of Fame? A .280 or maybe .300? If he was to have a batting average of .300, this means he would get a hit about one out of three tries. That is, he misses twice as much as he hits. He makes two mistakes for every three attempts, yet he becomes a Hall of Famer.

I once heard a story about a research engineer who lost over a million dollars on a project. When the CEO called him to his office, he asked the engineer what he had learned. After giving the CEO the lengthy details, the CEO thanked him and sent him on his way. As the engineer approached the door, he turned to the CEO and said, "You mean you're not going to fire me?" The CEO then replied, "Fire you? Son, I just spent a million dollars to educate you!"

As a successful leader you want your people to grow and to take risks. The best way to promote risk-taking is to allow mistakes. Remember, the turtle only makes progress when he sticks his neck out.

Study Questions

When you try something new, how do you approach it? Why?

How Do you feel when other people make a mistake that affects you?

Growth in an individual comes from_____.

How do you expect the people around you to respond to your mistakes?

How willing are you to take a risk ?

What is the biggest mistakes that you have ever made?

What makes risk taking easy for you?

PROGRESS NOTES

Commandment #7

BE ADAPTABLE AND PROACTIVE TO CHANGE

• •

"Have this attitude in yourselves which was also in Christ Jesus"
Philippians 2:5

Read: Psalm 103

CHANGE:

Change. A word that causes us to immediately become uncomfortable. Fear fills our minds. We are cautious and hesitate to approach it. We see it as adversity or even a threat. Why do most people view change in such a negative way?

It started when we were very young. We have been conditioned to respond this way. People like to feel that they are in control of their lives and when change occurs, that control is jeopardized.

As a leader, you will need to take a proactive approach to change. Research the facts, gather the data and anticipate what the change will bring. One of the most effective ways to be proactive to change is by planning. The very nature of planning makes you proactive. Without a plan, you are totally reactive, being satisfied with the status quo.

Being reactive is a dangerous course to take. You will be so busy trying to put out the many fires of the day, that you will lose sight of the important things that will help you and your organization progress. Planning will give the upper hand in life.

PLANNING:

Planning starts with scheduling a few minutes each day to determine what needs to be done. Make a list of all the things that you can think of that need to be accomplished. After the list is made, prioritize the list with those things that will impact you the most, being at the top. Now set out to accomplish as many items on the list as possible.

Now, most people will agree that unexpected situations do come up during the day. So in an effort to remain proactive, you should plan for such emergencies by planning only 65% of your day. This will give you time to work on those unexpected things that arise from time to time.

Daily planning must be based on weekly, monthly, yearly and lifetime plans. So when you are developing your plan, look ahead to see what can be done to impact your future. Most leaders have plans that go five years or more forward in time. The following diagram will help make this planning process easy.

Scope of Planning

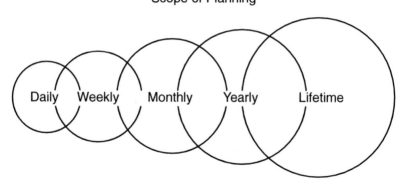

Anticipating Change:
Now, everyone knows that even the best plans can be destroyed by sudden and unexpected change. The best way to prevent your plans from being ruined is by trying to anticipate change before it occurs.

Anticipating change can be accomplished by keeping good communication lines open. Talk to people. Build networks. Share information. Know what the trends are and look for small or subtle changes in those trends. Gather as much information as possible and deal in facts, not assumptions. Analyze your data and alter your plans accordingly.

Information can also be gathered by reading books and magazines. Stay abreast of what's new and what's coming. Keep a constant finger on the pulse of your organization and your industry.

Anticipating change is not easy but by following these simple guidelines, you will be much more prepared for what change is coming and how you should deal with it.

ATTITUDE:
Being proactive and adaptable to change requires the right attitude. When unanticipated change comes, use the control that you have to deal with it. After that, adapt and accept the rest. This is much easier to accomplish when you have a positive attitude. You see, I believe that the attitude is the one thing that we have total control over. When I get up in the morning, I can choose to be positive and in a good mood or I can choose to be negative and in a bad mood. If I have this choice, then I choose to be positive.

Attitudes are very contagious. People will catch your attitude no matter if it's a good one or a bad one. As a leader, make sure you are spreading a positive attitude to the people.

If you approach your life with a positive frame of mind, you will notice that you are constantly looking for the good in things instead of the bad. What opportunity is presenting itself disguised as change or adversity? Without exception, every change and adversity has some opportunity linked to them. The secret is developing the type of an attitude that allows you to see the opportunity that is clouded by our old perceptions.

Here is a simple example. Let's say that you have planned a family picnic for several weeks. The food, the games and fellowship is being looked forward to by the whole family. The day comes and it is pouring down rain. You look at your wife and kids and you can see the disappointment all over their faces.

You're the leader and you have developed this positive attitude to be proactive and adaptable. You can't change the weather but you can adapt to it. Who says a picnic has to occur outside in the park? You make a few adjustments, present a positive outlook and announce the picnic is still on. Only we are changing the location to our basement. Spread out the blanket. Bring the food down and send the kids to get some games that everyone can play. Handled properly, I think everyone can help save the day. The key to success is how you, the leader, approach it.

Sure, this is a pretty simple example but the principle can be applied to any area of your life. Let's look at another example.

I had been working in a health care organization for twenty years. I was very much in my comfort zone and had planned to retire from this company in about twenty more years. Then something happened. By keeping my finger on the pulse of the organization, I started anticipating major changes over the horizon. Managed care was causing many health care organizations to downsize. I felt that my job would at some point be eliminated. So how could I beat change to the punch? What would I do if I lost my job? After all, I had been there for twenty years.

Keeping a positive attitude and maintaining a proactive approach, I decided to start my own training company. So I sat down and developed a plan of action. I developed goals, time frames, a budget, an operational plan and a marketing plan. Before long, the business was going well. I continued to do my best in my full time job but the business was keeping me busy as well.

Now I could have sat back and felt sorry for myself, blamed the company and thought how unfair it was for them to treat me this way. Instead, I chose to utilize the control that I had and made something happen. I walked away from the company with a very positive attitude and I continue to do some training for that company as well.

What started out as an adversity, turned quickly into an opportunity. Chances are, if change had not come, I would still be sitting in my "comfort zone" instead of doing what I love.

So I say to you, CYA (Change Your Attitude)! Start looking at change with a different perspective. See change as opportunity not adversity. Don't allow your past conditioning to influence your views on change. Respond with a take-charge attitude, utilizing whatever control that you have over the situation. You will find that you will be much more successful in the long run.

Thinking It Over

1. Evaluate your attitude today. Is it good or bad? Why?

2. How is your personal life? Positive or negative? Why?

3. How do you view your job? Positive or negative? Why?

4. Define success_____

   _____.

5. What is the difference between a problem and an opportunity?

6. How often do you work to help others to succeed?

7. Define that which is right.

8. What was your childhood like?

9. Who controls your attitude?

10. What thoughts and behaviors do you need to change?

PROGRESS NOTES

Commandment #8
LISTEN TO UNDERSTAND

• •

"Wise people will listen and learn more."
                                    Proverbs 1:5

Read: James 1:19-27

As a leader, you will be communicating a great deal. You may want to obtain information, coach, counsel, mentor, teach or delegate, all of which depends on effective communication.

Communication depends on two people. First, there is the sender or the individual who is conveying the message. The second is the receiver or the individual who is listening and receiving the message. If either party fails to carry out their part, then the communication will not be effective.

The sender must be clear in sending the message. He or she must use words that the receiver will understand and interpret as intended. Any confusion will result in poor communications. Here is an example.

Mary needs to assign a project to Bob. Mary approaches Bob and tells him that she needs him to do A, B, C. Bob says okay and leaves to carry out the assignment. When Mary follows up later, she finds that Bob did not do A, B, C. Instead, he did B, A, C. Did communication take place? Who's at fault for the assignment not being carried out properly?

Communication only takes place when the sender is sure that the receiver receives the information as it was intended. Obviously, Bob received the message differently than it was sent. Frequently, leaders will become upset that assignments are not carried out properly but many times this is due to the lack of effective communication.

Since Mary was the sender of the message, it was her responsibility to assure that the receiver had received the information as it was intended. This can usually be accomplished by asking questions and continuing the dialogue.

Communication is made up of three distinct parts. There is the words, the tone and the non-verbal parts. Words make up only 15% of effective communication, while the tone of voice makes up 35%. The most dominant part of communication, however, is the non-verbal or body language, which accounts for 50%.

Observe people when they talk. Do they maintain direct eye contact? Do they cross their arms? Do they appear nervous or relaxed? Are they calm or angry? Nonverbal communication is very strong no matter what form it comes in. Make sure you are communicating effectively and not being misinterpreted.

BARRIERS:

Many things can stand in the way of communication. I call them communication barriers.

Distractions such as noise, telephones and other people can completely stop communication. Try to find an environment that is quiet and will allow you to talk without interruptions.

Stop whatever you are doing and listen to the sender. Give them your full attention and let them know you are paying attention. Ask questions to confirm your understanding. This also shows that you care about the individual and their message.

As you listen to understand, make sure you don't assume you know the message before it is sent. Don't interrupt the sender by saying such things as, "I know what you are going to say." Respect the individual and their message.

When listening, make sure you are clear as to the meaning of the words being used. Words have many meanings and their meaning to you as an individual may depend on past experience or knowledge. In any case, don't jump to conclusions.

UNDERSTANDING NEEDS:

Listening to understand can also be accomplished by just staying in contact with the people. Idle conversation can keep you informed as to an individual's personal life. You may pick up on problems that they are having at work or at home.

Understanding individual needs is important for any leader. Not just those needs at work but in their life in general. The more you understand the people, the easier it is to work with them.

Good listening skills will also help build trust. If the people feel you really care and are trying to understand them, they will be much more likely to trust you. John Maxwell once said, "People don't care how much you know until they know how much you care." The best way to let them know you care is by listening and understanding their needs.

Trust is one of the most important aspects of leadership. Without trust, everyone is constantly looking over their backs to see who will be stabbing them next. You cannot stay a leader for long if the people don't trust you. Build trust levels by keeping the communication lines open. Let people say what they have on their minds. I would much rather have people venting their concerns and frustrations to me than to others in the organization. Try to address their concerns and you will have taken an important step in building a trusting relationship.

The Bible has a good lesson in this topic. James 1:19 states, "Be quick to listen, slow to speak and slow to anger."

PROGESS NOTES

Commandment #9

LINK RECOGNITION AND REWARDS TO PERFORMANCE

• •

"Do not withhold good from those who deserve it, when it is within your power to act."

Proverbs 3:27

Read: Philippians 2:1-18

Every organization has good performers and bad performers. As a leader, you must make it very clear which you prefer for your organization. Far too often, people are recognized for not performing up to par. This is done by simply ignoring poor performance. By doing nothing you send a clear message that poor performance is acceptable. After time the poor performance becomes the standard.

If you recognize and reward poor performance by ignoring it, you punish the people who are performing well. Think about it. Your good performers are being treated the same as a poor performer. Therefore, they are punished for doing a good job. Consider also the fact that the good performers have little for which they are motivated.

Strong and successful leaders will address poor performance quickly. They counsel, they coach and they take disciplinary actions when needed to correct performance. In doing so, they are firm, fair and consistent.

Recognizing positive behavior tends to motivate more positive behavior. Let people see that extra effort is recognized and you begin developing an environment in which people can motivate themselves.

There are many types of rewards and recognition that can be utilized at very little expense. A simple card or letter sent to an individual's home makes a very positive impact. The individual can share the card or letter with family members and additional support is received. Frequently, these cards and letters end up on the refrigerator with the kids' school papers.

From time to time you can place a gift certificate or lottery ticket in the card. Many retailers will donate gift certificates if they know it's being used as part of a reward system.

MAKE REWARDS AND RECOGNITION VISIBLE:

When you send a card to an employee's home, you make that recognition visible to the family members. This support is very important and meaningful for motivating continuous high performance.

If you are presenting rewards to an individual, make sure it is in front of peers. This helps reinforce the high standards that you expect from the members of the organization. Staff meetings or special banquets can be utilized to increase visibility.

DEFINE THE EXPECTATIONS:

Several organizations that I know of have made the mistake of giving out rewards with little or no guidelines. This practice will take away the value of such rewards. People need to know exactly what they must do for specific rewards.

Everyone in the organization gets a paycheck. That pay check is for performing at a certain level. If your organization is goal-oriented, that check may be for achieving certain goals but what happens when the baseline standards and goals are exceeded? That's when rewards need to be given.

If an individual is responsible for completing an assigned project by September 1st but he or she actually completes it by August 15th, that extra effort should be rewarded. When someone asks why the individual received the reward, it is very easy to explain the reason. Using rewards in this manners will help you increase the standards within your organization.

MAKE IT SINCERE:

A simple thank-you or pat on the back in front of peers goes a long way in recognizing good performance. If it is not done in a truly sincere manner, it can have a degrading effect on the individual.

The members of the organization must know that any reward or recognition given is done with sincerity and is in direct response to your appreciation for their contribution.

MAKE IT MEANINGFUL:

Rewards and recognition must be meaningful. If they have no meaning to the individual, they will have little or no affect in motivating them.

One company I know of never gives out cash rewards. Cash tends to be spent quickly and then forgotten. Instead of giving a $300 cash reward, this company will give an all-expense paid weekend for two at a nearby city. All meals, lodging and entertainment are paid for. Consider how much more meaning this reward has now that it is being shared with a spouse or friend.

This does not mean that cash rewards should never be given. It just means that frequently cash has less meaning and short term benefits.

MAKE IT UNIQUE:

Rewards need to be unique, different and should change from time to time. Rewards have more impact if the members of the organization don't know what to expect.

A small computer company contacted me recently and they were concerned that their reward system was loosing it's impact. After questioning them, I found that they had been giving t-shirts and sweatshirts out for the last three years as rewards. Needless to say, that after a few months of receiving t-shirts, they were no longer meaningful or unique.

I provided a list of possible changes in their reward system and after their first staff meeting, the program had new excitement and meaning. So make sure you change your rewards frequently. Make it a surprise. Make it exciting and make it sincere.

Depending on your budget, here are a few examples of rewards:

- Lottery tickets
- Gift certificates
- Dinner for two
- T-shirts
- Jackets
- Sweaters
- Lunch with the boss
- Weekend trip for two
- Plane tickets for two
- Pizza party
- Half or full day off with pay
- Cash
- Sporting event tickets
- Concert tickets
- Plaques
- Radio
- TVs
- Paid continuing education class
- Membership to a fitness club
- Free golf course green time
- Amusement park tickets for the family
- Free rental car for a month
- Free family portrait
- Savings bond
- Cellular phone or
- Free air time for existing cell phone
- 50 or 100 gallons of gasoline
- Free computer online service (1 month)
- Trip to the organization's national convention
- Flowers
- Books

These are just a few examples of the many rewards that can be given. Use your imagination and you can come up with many more.

Think About It

What motivates you?

What motivates the people around you?

What performance have you seen that needs rewarded?

When was the last time you caught someone doing something good?

PROGRESS NOTES

Commandment #10

PROMOTE WIN-WIN THINKING

• •

"Be united in the same mind and same judgment."
1 Cor. 1:10

Read. Acts 4:32-37

The successful leader must establish an environment of cooperation within the organization. Everyone must be committed to helping each other succeed. Selfish attitudes of "me" versus "them" are not conducive to a growing organization. Promoting a win-win attitude will help develop the cooperative atmosphere.

So what is win-win? Is it the same as compromise? Win-win is much different than compromise in that it provides a third solution to the situation. Normally, when two people have a disagreement, there are two possible solutions. Each party has an idea or view point as to how the problem should be resolved. This situation can lead to significant problems within the organization, such as conflict and bad attitudes.

Let's look at the following example. The supervisor of a small manufacturing company calls all the members of his department together for a meeting. He explains that they have received a very large order and it has to be shipped within five days. His calculations indicate that if everyone works two hours overtime, for the next four days, they can meet the deadline.

Now employees feel that instead of staying an additional two hours each day, they could just work eight hours on Saturday. Most of the employees have kids involved in activities in the evening and working an extra two hours would interfere with this.

The supervisor objects to working on Saturday because many of the machines in the work area are scheduled for a long overdue maintenance check. Working on Saturday would set the maintenance back further.

If the two parties in this scenario were to compromise, each would have to give up something. Each would lose to some extent.

However, if we begin thinking win-win, no one loses but both parties win. Win-win means we develop a new solution. A third solution that is different than the two currently on the table.

In this scenario, a third solution is suggested. What if we come in two hours early each day? The extra work is completed and the employees can still attend their kids' activities in the evening. The supervisor is happy because the deadline can still be met without working on Saturday, thus keeping the machine maintenance on schedule. Both parties win and no one has to lose.

In win-win situations, members of the organization strive to understand each others' problems and develop solutions that allow everyone to succeed.

Here's an interesting exercise to try. Place a strip of tape, about eighteen inches long, on the floor. Now pick two people and have them stand facing each other with the tape between them. Their instructions are simple. Each person is to convince the other to step over to his or her side of the line. Without using force, each person explains why it is best for the other person to cross over to their side.

We are so conditioned to thinking win-lose or compromise, most people will spend a significant amount of time trying to convince each other to cross the line. In a win-win thought process, both parties agree to trade places. The objective is met and everyone wins.

Developing a win-win thought process will help improve morale, stimulate innovation and build cooperation throughout the organization. Cooperation leads to success. When we work with others in a win-win process, we move closer to our goals.

Henry Ford said it this way, "Coming together is a beginning; staying together is a process; working together is success.

Leaders are not just born. Leaders are developed over time. Use these ten commandments by working on one each week. At the end of ten weeks, start over. Ask your friends how you're doing. Get feedback from the members of the organization but keep working at it. By changing your thought process and developing certain skills, anyone can become a highly successful leader.

"Be shepherds of God's flock that is under your care. Serving as overseers ... as God wants you to be ... not lording it over those entrusted to you, but being examples to the flock."

1 Peter 5:2 - 3
(NIV)

PROGRESS NOTES

ABOUT THE AUTHOR

Tim Holman is a Training and Development Specialist that has helped individuals and organizations across the nation to maximize their potential.

Tim is a member of the National Speakers Association, the American Society for Training and Development, the International Association of Fire Chiefs and the Fellowship of Christian Fire Fighters. He lives in West Central Ohio with Becky his wife and their three daughters Nikki, Jennifer and Michelle.

If you would like additional copies of **The Ten Commandments of Highly Successful Leaders** contact us by phone or write to us.

Please send:

————— Information about seminars on keynotes.

_____ copies of **The Ten Commandments of Highly Successful Leaders** @ $5.00 each $ _____

Postage and handling @ $2.50 per book $ _____

Ohio residents add 6% tax $ _____

Total amount enclosed $ _____

Ship to: (please print)

Name _____

Address _____

City, State, Zip _____

Day phone _____

Make checks payable to **Tim L. Holman**

Send to: P.O. Box 353
North Hampton, Ohio 45349
(937) 964-1534

- -

Please send:

————— Information about seminars on keynotes.

_____ copies of **The Ten Commandments of Highly Successful Leaders** @ $5.00 each $ _____

Postage and handling @ $2.50 per book $ _____

Ohio residents add 6% tax $ _____

Total amount enclosed $ _____

Ship to: (please print)

Name _____

Address _____

City, State, Zip _____

Day phone _____

Make checks payable to **Tim L. Holman**

Send to: P.O. Box 353
North Hampton, Ohio 45349
(937) 964-1534